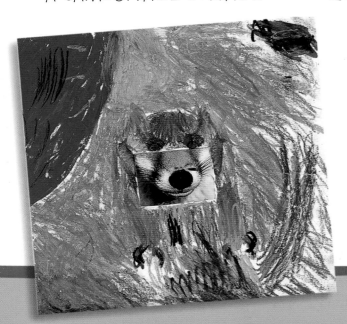

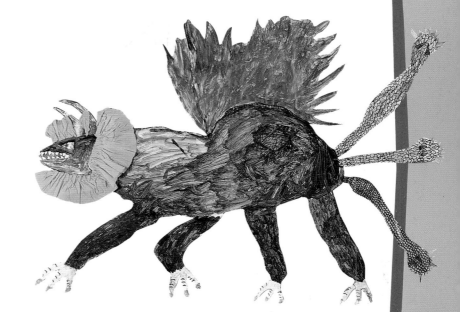

ANIMAL ALLSORTS

Creatures, both real and imaginary, have always fascinated artists. In this book we'll see how rich and varied animal life can be. We'll explore some of the different ways in which artists have depicted animals. You can find out what inspired the artists and learn about their techniques. There are also questions to help you look at the works in detail, and ideas for creating your own pictures and sculptures.

⦿ You'll find answers to the questions and information about the artists on pages 30-31.

Arty tips

✫ Look out for Arty tips boxes that suggest handy techniques and materials to use in your own work.

Picture hunt

✫ Picture hunt boxes suggest other artists and artworks that you might like to look at.

Lascaux cave painting (unknown artist)
Dordogne, France, c15,000 BC

Introducing animals

Some of the first pictures ever made were of animals. Stone Age artists painted lively images of cows, horses, bison and deer on the walls of dark caves. They used colours made by mixing together powdered rocks and plants with clay and water.

A First Look at Art

Creatures

Ruth Thomson

Chrysalis Children's Books

First published in the UK in 2003 by
Chrysalis Children's Books
An imprint of Chrysalis Books Group Plc
The Chrysalis Building, Bramley Road,
London W10 6SP

Paperback edition first published in 2005
Copyright © Chrysalis Books Group Plc 2003
Text copyright © Ruth Thomson 2003

ISBN 1 84138 704 5 (hb)
ISBN 1-84458-245-0 (pb)

British Library Cataloguing in Publication Data
for this book is available from the British Library.

Editorial manager: Joyce Bentley
Editor: Susie Brooks
Designers: Rachel Hamdi, Holly Mann
Picture researchers: ilumi, Aline Morley
Illustrator: Linda Francis
Photographer: Steve Shott
Consultant: Erika Langmuir

The author and publishers would like to thank
the following people for their contributions to this
book: Liz Burton, Clare Whyles and Saskia Van
der Zee and their pupils at St Ebbe's C.E. Primary
School, Oxford; Laycock Primary School, Islington;
Elizabeth Emerson; Rachel Petty; Leo Thomson.

Printed in China

Picture acknowledgements

Front cover: Estate of Eileen Agar; 4: Philidelphia Museum
of Art, Bequest of Lisa Norris Elkins; 5: Bridgeman Art
Library; 6: Bridgeman Art Library/© ADAGP, Paris and
DACS, London 2003; 6: Bridgeman Art Library/© Succession
Picasso/DACS; 10: Estate of Eileen Agar; 15: Gift of Mr and
Mrs Klaus G Perls, © 2003 Board of Trustees, National
Gallery of Art Washington/ARS, NY and DACS, London
2003; 18/19: AKG London/National Gallery of Art,
Washington; 22/23: Gift of Mrs Richard E Danielson and
Mrs Chauncey McCormick, 1933.786, reproduction, The
Art Institute of Chicago; 26/27: AKG London/Albright-Knox
Art Gallery, Buffalo (NY)/© Succession Miro, DACS, 2003.

Contents

Noah's Ark
Edward Hicks
1846 (66.8 x 77.2cm)

Telling tales

Animal paintings often tell us stories. This one illustrates a scene from the Bible, when creatures fled in pairs to the Ark to escape the coming flood.

Artists in some ancient civilisations depicted imaginary creatures that were described in their myths. Others made symbols of real creatures that they admired or feared. Bulls and lions, for example, represented strength and power.

Animal artists

Throughout history, many forms of animal art have developed. Some artists have been with explorers to distant countries, painting and drawing the wildlife they've seen. Some have painted animal scenes to hang on the walls of people's homes. Other artists have made their living painting portraits or creating sculptures of people's favourite pets.

The Cat
Tsuguharu Foujita
1927
(38 x 46cm)

The way that something feels to the touch is called texture. Artists can suggest textures by using different lines, shapes, light and dark.

Lines can be fine or heavy, solid or broken. Shapes can be curvy or jagged. The use of light and dark may suggest shine, softness, sharpness or roughness.

Soft and furry

The body of this pet cat was drawn with lots of short lines. These suggest the soft texture of fur. The lines are gently blended with a thin layer, or wash, of ink.

◉ Which parts of the cat are drawn with a solid line?

◉ How would these parts feel compared with the rest?

Sharp and scary

Picasso liked street cats because they are cunning, skilful hunters. His painting shows how fierce and fearless these animals can be.

This cat's bold, solid outline makes it look tense and alert. Its back is arched, its tail is stiff and upright and its front leg sticks out at a sharp angle.

Picasso has used blocks of solid colour, which add to the aggressive feel of the painting.

◉ Which parts of this cat make it look very menacing?

◉ How has Picasso emphasised that cats have keen eyesight?

◉ If you could touch the cats in these two pictures, how would they feel? Think of three words to describe each one.

Cat and Bird
Pablo Picasso
1939
(97 x 130cm)

7

MAKING MARKS

Lines and textures

Practise making different sorts of marks using soft pastels, coloured pencils and felt-tips. Make long, flowing marks, scratchy scribbles, strong, crisp lines and short, soft ones.

Cat surprise!

◉ Fold a sheet of paper into three, as shown below.

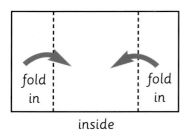

fold in · inside · fold in

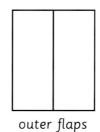

outer flaps

◉ Decide whether the cat inside will be fierce or friendly. On the outer flaps, draw some textured marks that give clues about its character.

◉ Inside, draw the cat, again using marks that suggest its personality.

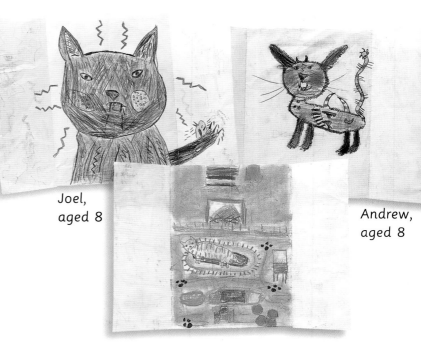

Joel, aged 8

Andrew, aged 8

Zahra, aged 8

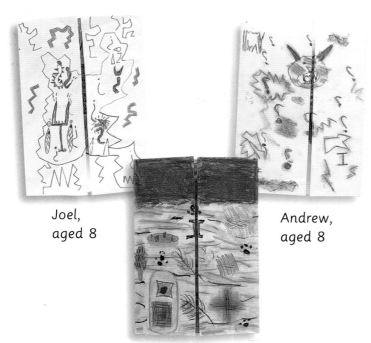

Joel, aged 8

Andrew, aged 8

Zahra, aged 8

Arty tips

✫ Use pastels and soft pencils (5B or 6B) for making soft, smudgy textures.

✫ Use hard pencils (HB), rollerball pens and coloured pencils for making sharper, more precise marks.

Two-faced cats

◉ Draw the outline of a cat's head on stiff card and cut it out.

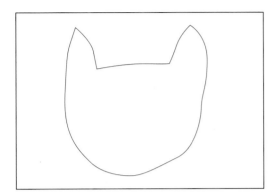

◉ Draw around this head on to another piece of card to create a second, identical outline.

◉ Cut this out.

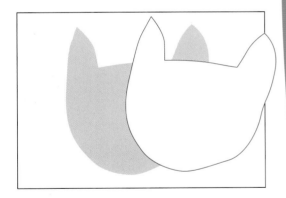

◉ Use paints, felt-tips or wax crayons to create one friendly and one fierce cat face.

Inez, aged 8

◉ Use soft colours and smudgy marks for the friendly cat.

David, aged 9

Daniel, aged 8

Eleri, aged 8

friendly

◉ Use bold outlines and strong colours for the fierce cat.

Zamir, aged 8

Aubrey, aged 8

Aaron, aged 9

fierce

◉ Glue the two faces back to back with a lolly stick between them.

Picture hunt

✪ Many other artists, such as Théodore Géricault, Paul Klee, Franz Marc and Pierre Auguste Renoir, painted cats. Find some of their images of cats and decide whether these artists saw cats as soft, gentle pets or as wild, aggressive animals.

NATURE'S PATTERNS

Artists often create pictures to express ideas that interest them. Eileen Agar was intrigued by the way new life begins and changes from one stage to another.

In this work, she explores how a bird develops. It grows inside an egg, until it is ready to hatch. Then tap! tap! tap! The bird cracks the eggshell and pops out. Once it is old enough, the bird may lay new eggs of its own.

Bird beginnings

This colourful bird leaps out from the page. Its clear, crisp form is as flat as a cardboard cut-out.

Agar overlapped two large egg forms with the bird to show how eggs become birds and birds, in their turn, lay eggs. The egg on the left looks cracked.

Maybe the bird has come out of the cracked egg, or is it still waiting to hatch inside the other one?

◉ Can you see any other hints of egg shapes?

Playful patterns

Agar filled her picture with different patterns. Some of them remind us of feathers. Others look like broken eggshell or nesting twigs.

◉ Can you spot all these patterns? What part of a bird do they remind you of?
● zig-zags
● circles
● checks
● stripes
● chevrons (V shapes)
● crazy paving shapes

◉ Find colours which are repeated on different parts of the bird and some that are used only once. How has Agar made the bird stand out?

The Bird
Eileen Agar
1969
(102 x 128cm)

DECORATIVE DISPLAYS

Pattern practice

◉ Fold a square of paper four times to make sixteen little squares.

◉ Draw a different pattern inside each square. Use your ideas to decorate a bird.

A beautiful bird

◉ Draw a bird shape on white paper and cut it out.

◉ Cover the bird with patterns, using felt-tip pens or paints.

◉ Glue the bird on to a contrasting coloured background, to make it really stand out.

◉ Add some extra decorative details all around the bird.

Picture hunt

✿ Compare Agar's work with pictures by other artists, such as Gustave Klimt, Henri Matisse and Sonia Delauney-Terk, which often include a great many patterns.

✿ Look at works by M C Escher, who often changed one shape, such as a fish, into another, such as a bird.

Emily, Suzie, Flora, Zak and Martha, all aged 8

A hatching egg

◉ Cut out an egg shape in card. Cut this in half, using a jagged line.

◉ Stick colourful pieces of paper all over both halves. Then glue the two halves on to a coloured card background, leaving a space between them for a bird.

◉ Make the bird from torn newspaper or coloured magazine pages. Stick it on to the card, as if it is hatching from the egg.

Zahra, Rowan, Alex, Lottie, Luke, Andrew, George and Aonghus, all aged 8

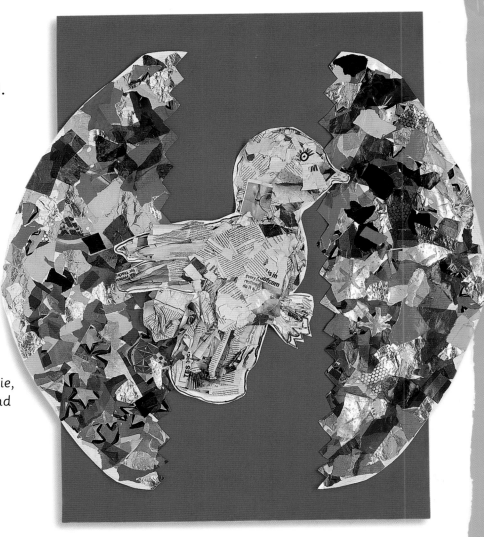

Eggcellent ornaments

◉ Ask an adult to help you hard-boil some eggs.

◉ When the eggs are completely cool and dry, paint them all over with bright patterns (see Arty tips).

Natasha, Hannah,
Grace, Helen, James and Josh, all aged 9

Arty tips

✰ It's easiest if you paint one end of your egg, then let it dry *before* painting the other end. That way you can always hold the egg without smudging any paint.

✰ You can use almost any kind of paint. When it's dry, add a coat of varnish for extra shine. You could try painting your egg with clear glue and rolling it in glitter.

✰ Hard-boiled eggs won't last for ever. For a more permanent ornament, use a smooth pebble or modelling clay.

CREATURES IN MOTION

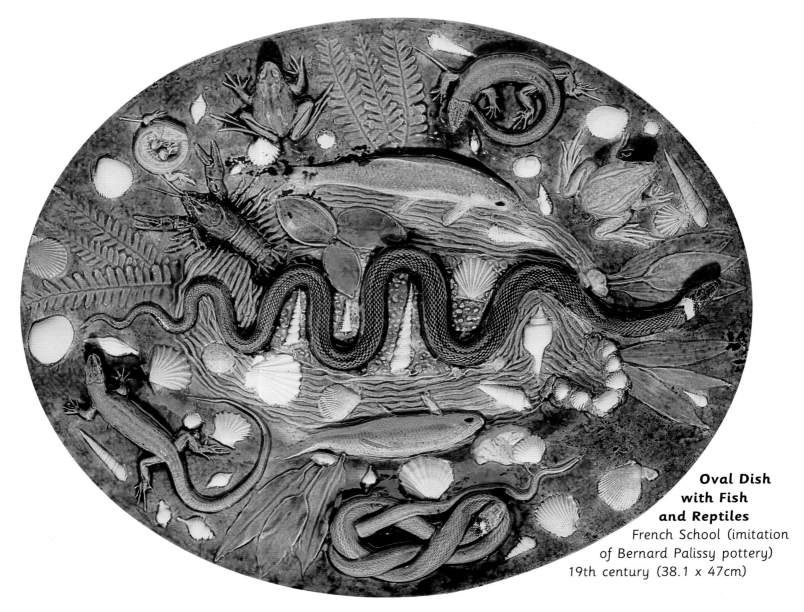

Oval Dish with Fish and Reptiles
French School (imitation of Bernard Palissy pottery) 19th century (38.1 x 47cm)

Animals may slither, slink or squirm. Some twist, twirl or twitch. Others wriggle, creep, crawl, gallop or glide. Artists can capture movements like these in different ways.

A pond on a plate

The bodies and tails of the creatures on this pottery plate bend, curve and curl this way and that, to suggest that they have been caught mid-action.

The potter has arranged the animals carefully, so that they don't touch or overlap one another.

⊙ Think of words to describe the way each of these creatures might move:
- the snake
- the frog and toad
- the fish
- the lizards
- the crayfish

Swimming in the air

This fish sculpture *really* moves. It hangs from the ceiling on a wire and swings gently to and fro in the faintest breeze. Moving sculptures like this are called mobiles. They were invented by Alexander Calder, who made this fish.

Shapes and scales

Notice how Calder bent strong wire into the outline of a fish. He filled this with a fine network of scale shapes and tied on dangling bits and pieces. As the objects twirl, they catch the light and glisten and shimmer.

Bits and pieces

Calder used all sorts of shiny oddments for the fish scales.

- See if you can spot:
  - a key
  - metal strainers
  - pieces of mirror
  - a metal funnel
  - coloured glass fragments
  - pottery pieces
  - spiral shapes
  - coloured wire
- Imagine seeing the fish on a sunny day. Which *bits and pieces* would glint and sparkle?

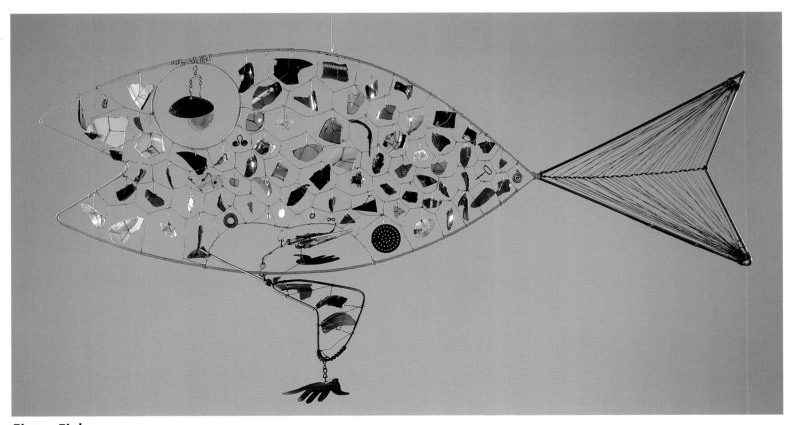

Finny Fish
Alexander Calder
1948 (66 x 152.4cm)

MODELLING MOVEMENT

A watery world

Transform a paper plate or plastic tray into a mini world, teeming with wildlife.

◉ Paint the plate blue, with streaky ripples.

◉ Make wriggling fish, a thrashing squid, a flapping turtle and other moving creatures from coloured modelling clay.

Farhaan, aged 9, and Mahliqa, aged 8

◉ Arrange the creatures on the plate or tray.

◉ Glue on some real seashells.

◉ You might like to add some green raffia seaweed, as well.

Dan and Nancy-Luz, both aged 8

◉ For a shimmery water effect, cover the tray or plate with clingfilm or clear cellophane.

Arty tips

✿ If you want to suggest that the creatures are moving, show them with one or more raised legs, waving antennae, or a twisting or curved body.

Marvellous mobiles

◉ Make your own mobile by twisting together lengths of thin garden wire.

◉ Thread on shiny beads, tinsel balls or sparkly sequins as you construct your creature, or attach feathers, pipe cleaners and pieces of shiny paper once the creature is complete.

Luke, aged 8, and Harry, aged 9

Yasmine, aged 8

◉ Hang your mobile somewhere where it can catch the light and turn in the breeze.

Sculpture hunt

✫ Look for pictures of other mobiles made by Calder. Many are made up of simple, brightly coloured shapes that hang from different 'arms', at varying heights.

✫ Find out about the works of Jean Tinguely, who also made moving sculptures from everyday objects.

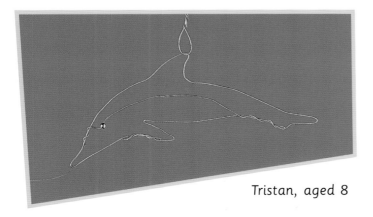

Tristan, aged 8

COLOUR AND CAMOUFLAGE

Wild animals are good at hiding. They lurk among leaves and bend around branches. Artists can play with camouflage to create surprises. Beware!

◉ What can you *see* hiding here? What might you hear?

◉ If you were in this forest, where and how would you hide?

The colours

Rousseau used many different shades of green when he painted this forest. The pale green and yellow in the background make it feel hot and steamy. The colours of the animals help them to hide. They sometimes blend in with the leaves and flowers.

◉ How many different greens can you find?

◉ Can you *see* colours that match animals to plants?

Leaves and flowers

Notice how every leaf and flower is crisply painted and clearly separate from the others next to it.

◉ How many differently shaped leaves and flowers can you spot?

Inspirations

Rousseau painted many tropical scenes like this one. He claimed that he had visited tropical forests when he was with the French army in Mexico. This was a fib. In fact, he imagined them, using photos and books as reference. He also spent a great deal of time sketching tropical plants and wild animals at the plant gardens in Paris.

◉ What is odd about the two monkeys in the foreground of this imaginary scene?

Tropical Forest with Monkeys
Henri Rousseau
1910 (129.5 x 162.5cm)

IN THE WILD

Complete the animal

◉ Cut out one important detail of an animal, such as its nose, teeth, scales or ears, from a magazine photograph.

◉ Glue it on to a piece of paper.

◉ Paint the rest of the animal around it.

◉ Include a background that shows where the animal lives.

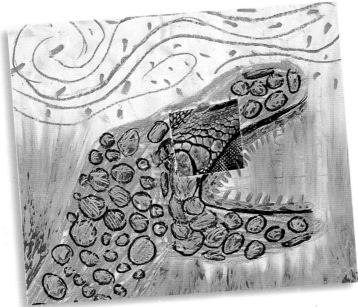

Maddy, aged 8

Martha, aged 8

A monkey mask

◉ Cut a circle of stiff card, or use a paper plate, for a monkey face.

◉ Glue on scrumpled balls of newspaper for a muzzle, cheeks and brow.

◉ Put several layers of newspaper strips, dipped in PVA and water, all over the face. Leave it to dry.

◉ Paint the face with monkey features. Glue on some woolly fur.

◉ Make separate paper ears and staple these to the monkey's head.

Kieran, aged 9

Picture hunt

✿ Find other rainforest pictures by Rousseau, such as *Virgin Forest at Sunset*, *The Dream*, *The Snake Charmer* and *Tiger in a Tropical Storm (Surprised!)*.

✿ Compare Rousseau's tropical forest picture with woodland paintings by Charles Burchfield, Emily Carr or Gustav Klimt.

Colour mixing

Make some different greens.

◉ Mix together equal amounts of blue and yellow.

◉ Mix more blue than yellow and more yellow than blue.

◉ Add a little white to your mixtures to make lighter tints.

◉ Add a little black or red to make darker shades.

A green jungle

◉ Use all the greens you have mixed to make a lush rainforest picture.

◉ Include some brightly coloured animals, snakes and birds, that stand out against the leafy background.

George, aged 9, and Aaron, aged 8

Joseph, aged 9, and Tristan, aged 8

A camouflage collage

◉ Make a rainforest collage, using strips of torn paper, crumpled tissue and corrugated card.

◉ Hide some animals and birds among the leaves, in the water or under fallen branches.

A MYTHICAL BEAST

Saint George Killing the Dragon
Bernardo Martorell
1430/35
(155.3 x 98cm)

Some creatures, such as dragons, do not exist in real life. But artists often make them up out of various parts of real animals, such as mammals, birds and reptiles.

◉ What types of animal has this artist used for the head, body, tail, wings and feet of his dragon?

The tale of Saint George

This picture tells the story of a dragon who terrorised a city kingdom. To keep it away, people gave it sheep to eat. When there were no sheep left, people drew lots each day to decide who would be the dragon's next victim. One day the lot fell on the princess.

In the nick of time, Saint George rode by and killed the dragon.

◉ Notice how the artist has included all details of the story. Look for:

- the city and the worried people
- a sheep and the princess
- skulls and bones of victims
- the dragon and his cave
- Saint George

MAKING MONSTERS

A monster poster

◉ Paint a detailed picture of a monster in eye-catching colours.

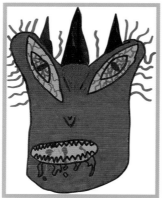

◉ Glue the picture on to a piece of contrasting coloured card and draw a frame around it.

◉ Write **WANTED** in big letters at the top of the card.

Picture hunt

✪ Try to find pictures of other strange beasts that are made up of a mixture of animals. Look for a gryphon, a chimera, a cockatrice, a hippocampus and an amphisbaena, for example.

WANTED
Grendel for murder! Terrorising! cannibalism! attacks!

DESCRIPTION: huge, mean, slimy, many-eyed
REWARD: bag of gold

Keeley, aged 9

WANTED
Grendel for killing people

DESCRIPTION: red-eyed, blue-hair, horned, two-nosed
REWARD: one million

Aymen, aged 8

◉ Give the monster's name.

◉ Say why it is wanted.

◉ Under its picture, describe the monster's main features.

◉ Offer a big reward!

Monster mix

◉ Draw a sketch of a monster made up from parts of several real animals. Think about the useful features of different animals — such as their wings, teeth, feet and necks.

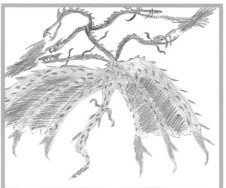

Daniel, aged 9

Think of answers to these questions about your monster. Include some of these details in your work:

◉ How does it move — can it fly, swim, jump or run fast?

Luc, aged 8, and Jack and Joseph, both aged 9

◉ Where does it live — in the sea, inside a volcano, on a mountaintop, in the desert or in a cave?

◉ What does it eat — plants, people or other animals?

◉ Is it colourful? Does it have any patterning or texture?

Arty tips

✫ To make a monster look really scary, exaggerate the size of its eyes, teeth, claws or horns.

✫ To emphasise a monster's strength, size or a particular ability, make its head, neck, body, wings or legs stand out.

Eleri and Ellie, both aged 8

Artists can paint whatever creatures they can imagine. Miró said that staring at cracks in his walls helped give him ideas for these fantastic creatures.

Party time

The Harlequin (the figure with a blue and red face) is having a noisy party with some unusual guests.

◉ Discover:
- a bird with a bow and arrow body
- three or more floating creatures
- two or more winged creatures
- a red-faced cat
- creatures with flower heads

◉ What other creatures can you find?

The Harlequin's Carnival
Joan Miró
1924-25 (66 x 93cm)

A carnival dance

The picture is filled with lively music and dancing.

Spot the musician with his guitar, some musical notes and a large ear listening from the ladder.

Notice how the shapes of the creatures suggest different movements.

◉ Which creatures sway, writhe or bounce to the music?

The colours

The party is in a bare room. The plain wall and floor make the colourful creatures stand out.

Miró makes the same shades of blue, red and yellow dance rhythmically across the picture.

JUST IMAGINE

Blotty creatures

◉ Fold a piece of paper in half and make a crease along the fold. Open the paper out again.

◉ Put several different coloured blobs of paint on one half of the paper.

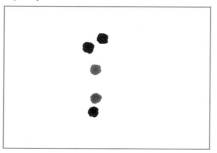

◉ Fold the paper in half again. Rub it, so that the blobs inside squish on to both sides of the paper. Open the paper out again and let the paint dry.

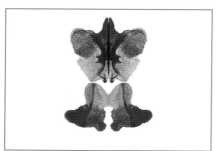

◉ What sort of creature do the blots suggest to you? Use a pen, felt-tips or paint to transform the blots into a strange animal.

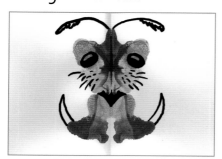

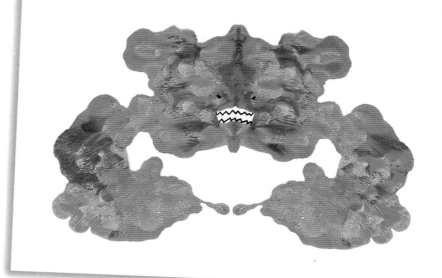

Louise, aged 9

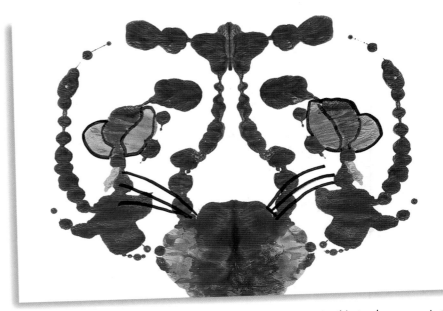

Natasha, aged 9

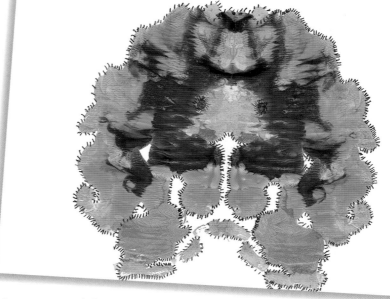

Rowan, aged 8

28

Crazy creations

◉ Use coloured modelling clay to make some strange creatures and create your own party or parade.

◉ Will your creatures have one eye, lots of eyes or none at all?

◉ Will they have feet or tails or will they wobble about on a round base?

◉ Will they have arms, paws or wings or none of these?

◉ Will they be plainly coloured, stripy or patterned?

Picture hunt

✦ Make a collection of paintings or drawings of imaginary creatures by other 20th-century artists, such as: Max Ernst, Paul Klee and Mervyn Peake.

Joe, aged 9

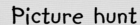

Imran, aged 9

Holly, aged 8

Amy, aged 8

Leo, aged 8

Dan, aged 9

David, aged 9

◉ Give each creature a name and make up a story about them.

ARTISTS AND ANSWERS

ANIMAL ALLSORTS (pages 4/5)

About the LASCAUX CAVES

The Lascaux caves were discovered in 1940 by four boys who were out walking. The cave walls are covered with nearly 600 paintings and engravings of animals, which date back to around 15,000 BC. Many are hunting scenes, typical of Stone Age times.

About EDWARD HICKS

Hicks (1780-1849) was a self-taught American artist, who began his career by painting coaches and signs. He was very religious and painted hundreds of pictures inspired by verses in the Bible.

TEXTURE AND TEMPER (pages 6/7)

Answers for page 6

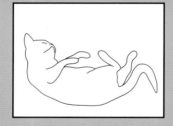

• The cat's ears, nose, mouth and leg joint are all painted with a solid line.
• These parts would feel harder than its furry body.

About TSUGUHARU FOUJITA

Foujita (1886-1968) was born in Japan and studied art at the Imperial School for Fine Arts in Tokyo. In 1913, he moved to Paris to learn more from European artists. He travelled widely, especially in North and South America. His landscapes, portraits and cats are painted in a delicate way, combining traditional Japanese and modern European styles. He also painted the walls of a chapel in Reims, in northern France.

Answers for page 7

• The sharp teeth and claws and the lined brow look menacing.
• Picasso emphasised the cat's eyes with several circles.
• Foujita's cat is soft, relaxed and furry; Picasso's is angular, tense and tight.

About PABLO PICASSO

Picasso (1886-1968) was probably the most famous artist of the 20th century. He was born in Spain, the son of an art teacher, and he showed a talent for art as a child. He studied in Barcelona and Madrid, then lived mainly in France. Picasso experimented with many ways of painting and sculpting. With his artist friend Georges Braque, he developed a new art style called Cubism. He made collages and sculptures from found objects, designed ballet sets and made etchings. He learned how to weld, cut and fold metal to make sculptures, painted pottery and made plaster models.

NATURE'S PATTERNS (pages 10/11)

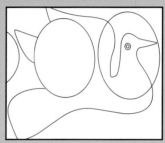

Answers for page 10

• There is a small blue egg under the curve of the bird's body. Parts of other eggs are hinted at elsewhere in the background.
• Zig-zags are on the eggs, the bird's neck and tail and in the top background. The bird's eye is two circles. There are checks below the bird and stripes on the bird's head, wing tip and tail. Chevrons are on the bird's chest and on one egg. There are green and pink crazy paving shapes on the eggs.
• Red, very deep pink, deep pink and strong orange are used only once. All the other colours are repeated. The bird stands out because it is painted in light, bright colours against a dark background.

About EILEEN AGAR

Agar (1899-1991) was a British artist. She was born in Buenos Aires in Argentina, but moved with her family to England in 1911. She studied art in London and spent several years in Paris, where she was influenced by an art style called Surrealism. Surrealist artists were interested in dreams, chance and the unconscious mind. Agar was also fascinated by nature, particularly the shapes of plants, shells, fossils and eggs. She created collages from found objects as well as painting pictures.

CREATURES IN MOTION (pages 14/15)

Answer for page 14

- Snakes wriggle, slither, slip and slide; fish dive, twist, skim and glide; crayfish crawl, wriggle and swim; frogs and toads jump or leap; lizards slink, climb, dash and scuttle.

About BERNARD PALISSY

Palissy (c1510-1590) – the artist who inspired this dish – was a French potter. Palissy made moulds from real objects, such as shells and dead fish. He laid the shapes on dishes, which were then fired and glazed.

Answer for page 15

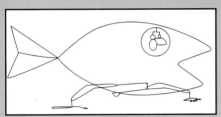

- The mirrors and glass would glisten and sparkle most in sunlight. There would also be reflections from the shiny metal and pottery parts.

About ALEXANDER CALDER

Calder (1898-1976) was an American who trained as an engineer before becoming a sculptor. His early works were wire portraits of celebrities, wire and wooden animals and a moving miniature wire circus. As well as inventing both hanging and standing mobiles, Calder made moving sculptures that were powered by either hand or motor. His later works were huge metal sculptures for public places.

COLOUR AND CAMOUFLAGE (pages 18/19)

Answers for pages 18 and 19

- There are five monkeys and a snake hiding in the painting.
- There are at least seven different greens.
- Some monkeys match the yellow flowers. The grey snake and monkeys match branches.
- There are at least seven differently shaped leaves and two types of flower.
- The monkeys are fishing with rods.

About HENRI ROUSSEAU

Rousseau (1844-1910) was a self-taught French painter. He served in the army and then worked as a customs officer in Paris. After he retired, he started painting portraits, scenes of everyday life and flowers, as well as imaginary, dream-like scenes, set in exotic surroundings. Rousseau was admired by Picasso, who organised a banquet in his honour.

A MYTHICAL BEAST (pages 22/23)

Answer for page 23

- The dragon has the hairy head of a wolf, the scaly body and tail of a reptile, the wings of a bat and the sharp claws of a bird of prey.

About BERNARDO MARTORELL

Martorell (c1400-1452) came from Spain and worked mainly in Barcelona. He is known for his painted altarpieces and miniatures.

IMAGINARY CREATURES (pages 26/27)

Answer for page 27

- The floating creatures with long tails, the Harlequin and the faceless white creature are all swaying; the white snake-like creature is writhing; the creatures on the floor and the springed creature in the air (top centre) are bouncing.

About JUAN MIRÓ

Miró (1893-1983) – a Spanish artist – studied art in Barcelona. He then went to Paris and met Picasso, who helped him exhibit his work. Miró's early paintings were very detailed, based on things he saw, but often arranged oddly and painted in strange colours. Later his paintings became simpler and more dream-like. People, creatures and objects are hinted at by odd shapes and sometimes words or symbols are included. Miró also made brightly coloured sculptures.

GLOSSARY

camouflage Blending in with your surroundings.

collage A picture made by sticking bits of paper, fabric, or other objects, on to a background.

Cubism A 20th-century art style, developed by Pablo Picasso and Georges Braque, in which artists broke down subjects into geometric shapes.

etching A form of print-making in which the artist scratches an image on to a metal plate. Ink is worked into the scratched marks, then the plate is pressed on to paper to print.

miniatures Very small, detailed paintings.

pastels Soft crayons that can be chalky (soft pastels) or oily (oil pastels).

texture How something feels to the touch, for example rough or smooth.

tints Light tones of a colour, often made by adding white.

wash A layer of thin, watery paint or ink.

INDEX